BAKING WITH HOMEPRIDE FLOUR

Colour Library Books

HOMEPRIDE FLOUR

An Introduction by Fred

Dear Friends,

I'd like to introduce you to this special recipe book, packed full of easy-to-follow, illustrated recipes for you to make using Homepride Flour.

Homepride Flour has been available for over 25 years, with generations of flour graders making sure that the grains are graded to make the finest flour possible – for the best baking results every time.

Homepride continue to produce a full range of flours for all your baking needs. The Self Raising and Plain varieties are now packed in a unique 1kg "stay-fresh" pack as well as in the traditional 1.5kg and 500g bags. This makes the flour easier to handle and convenient to store – designed to make baking with Homepride even simpler than ever! In addition, the Harvest Gold range of bread flours and yeast will allow you to make loaves of crusty bread that everyone will love.

All the recipes in this book have been thoroughly kitchen-tested at Homepride and will suit a range of occasions from dinner parties to family meals and teatime snacks – all "Homemade with Homepride"!

Allow me to take you through them . . .

Happy Baking!
Fred

CLB 2687
© 1991 Colour Library Books Ltd., Godalming, Surrey.
Printed in Singapore.
All rights reserved.
ISBN 0 86283 870 3

Homepride and the Homepride man device are the registered
trademarks of Dalgetty Foods Ltd.

WHOLEMEAL BREAD

Makes one small 450g (1lb) loaf and five rolls, or one large loaf

A classic bread, perfect for sandwiches.

325g/12 oz Harvest Gold Wholemeal Flour
150g/5oz Harvest Gold Strong White Flour
5g/1 tsp salt
15g/½oz white vegetable fat
12g/2 sachets Homepride Easy Blend Yeast
300ml/11 fl oz water (150ml near boiling,
    150ml cold)

Glaze
1 egg, size 3, lightly beaten
50ml/2 fl oz milk
2.5g/½ tsp salt

1. Preheat oven to 230°C/450°F/Gas Mark 8.

2. Grease a small loaf tin and baking tray or, for a large loaf, a 1kg (2lb) loaf tin.

3. Mix together the flours and salt and rub in the fat. Add yeast.

STEP 3

4. Blend in the water and mix to form a soft dough.

5. Turn out onto a lightly floured surface and knead for about 5 minutes to give a smooth dough.

Shape or mould as required, placing moulded joins downwards ready for baking.

6. Beat together the egg with the milk and salt and glaze the shaped dough. Cover with lightly oiled cling film and prove in a warm place until double in size.

STEP 5

7. Remove cling film, re-glaze and bake the rolls for 10 minutes, the small loaf for 15 to 20 minutes or the large loaf for 20 to 30 minutes until well risen and golden brown.

8. Turn out onto a wire rack and re-glaze immediately with the egg mixture to give a shiny appearance. Allow to cool before slicing.

STEP 7

Cook's Notes

⏲ TIME: Preparation takes about 25 minutes, baking takes up to 30 minutes.

📖 COOK'S TIP: To keep dough warm during proving, place the tins into an insulation container until fully risen. If all wholemeal flour is used, extra water may be needed.

JAM DOUGHNUTS

MAKES 12

All age groups appreciate these traditional tea-time treats.

500g/1lb 2oz Harvest Gold Strong White Flour
25g/1oz margarine
25g/1oz caster sugar
12g/2 sachets Homepride Easy Blend Dried Yeast
300ml/11 fl oz water (150ml near boiling, 150ml cold)
200g/7oz jam

Coating
100g/3½oz granulated sugar
5g/1 tsp ground cinnamon

1. Sieve the flour into a large mixing bowl and rub in the margarine. Stir in the sugar and dried yeast.

2. Mix in the warm water, stirring continuously with a round bladed knife until well blended together.

STEP 2

3. Turn the dough out onto a lightly floured surface and knead for about 5 minutes until smooth.

4. Divide the dough into pieces of about 65g (2½oz), knead into a small round and roll out each to about 10cm (4 inches) in diameter.

5. Place rounded teaspoons of jam in the centre of the rounds of dough, lightly dampen the edges with a little water and draw the dough together carefully over the jam. Seal well, turn over, and place on a tray and cover with lightly oiled cling film. Prove in a warm place until double their size.

STEP 5

6. Meanwhile heat the oil for frying to 185°C/375°F. When the doughnuts have risen, place smooth side down in the hot oil and fry for 2 to 2½ minutes on each side until golden brown.

STEP 6

7. Drain the doughnuts on absorbent paper and then roll in the sugar and cinnamon which have been mixed together.

Cook's Notes

🕐 TIME: Preparation takes 40 minutes, frying takes 5 minutes.

◎ SERVING IDEAS: Cut doughnuts through the 'waist line' and fill with fresh or butter cream.

EGG CUSTARD TART

An old favourite which is still enjoyed today.

Pastry
175g/6oz Homepride Plain Flour
75g/3oz butter
1 egg yolk
15g/1 tbsp caster sugar
30ml/2 tbsps cold water

Egg Custard
275ml/½ pint milk
2 eggs, size 3
Egg white from pastry above
50g/2 oz caster sugar
Grated nutmeg to taste

1. Preheat the oven to 200°C/400°F/Gas Mark 6.

2. Sieve the flour into a bowl and rub in the butter.

3. Mix together the egg yolk with the caster sugar and add to the rubbed in mixture with the water, to form a soft dough.

STEP 5

4. Turn out onto a lightly floured surface and knead gently until smooth and silky. Roll out the pastry to fit a 20cm (8-inch) flan ring placed on a baking tray.

5. Lift the pastry carefully on the rolling pin and ease into the ring without breaking. Press smoothly round sides and bottom. Cut off surplus pastry with a sharp knife.

6. Line inside of pastry case with a round of greaseproof paper and arrange baking beans or crusts of bread on top to prevent pastry rising. Bake in preheated oven for 10-15 minutes, then remove greaseproof paper and baking beans.

7. Turn oven down to 160°C/325°F/Gas Mark 3.

8. To prepare the egg custard, warm the milk slightly. Lightly whisk the eggs with the egg white from the pastry, and the sugar. Pour in the milk and stir together. Strain through a sieve into the baked pastry case and sprinkle the surface with ground nutmeg.

STEP 8

9. Bake for 35 minutes until the custard has set. Be careful not to overbake as the custard will curdle.

Cook's Notes

TIME: Preparation takes 25 minutes, cooking takes 50 minutes.

COOK'S TIP: Always keep the same dried peas or beans for blind baking pastry cases. Store in airtight containers.

VIENNESE FANCIES

Makes about 18

These light, sweet biscuits are very simple to make.

275g/10oz butter
50g/2oz icing sugar
275g/10oz Homepride Plain Flour
Vanilla essence to taste
Paper cases

1. Preheat the oven to 200°C/400°F/Gas Mark 6.

2. Place 18 paper baking cases in a sheet of patty tins or on a baking sheet.

3. Cream the butter with the icing sugar until light and fluffy.

STEP 3

4. Gradually add the flour with a few drops of vanilla essence, and beat well between each flour addition.

STEP 5

5. Put the mixture into a piping bag fitted with a large star nozzle. Pipe the mixture into the paper cases, starting in the middle and piping with a spiral motion round the sides.

6. Bake in the centre of preheated oven for about 15 minutes, until light golden in colour.

7. Leave in their paper cases to cool on a wire rack. Sprinkle with sieved icing sugar.

Cook's Notes

⏱ TIME: Preparation takes 15 minutes, baking takes 15 minutes.

👨‍🍳 COOK'S TIP: If no piping bag is available, the mixture may be spooned into the cases and levelled with the back of the spoon.

◯ SERVING IDEAS: As an attractive finish, after sprinkling with icing sugar, stick half a glace cherry in the centre with jam and one or more small diamonds of angelica radiating out from the cherry to represent leaves.

FRESH CREAM RASPBERRY SCONE DESSERT

A delectable cake which is sure to impress your guests.

Scone base
225g/8oz Homepride Self-Raising Flour
50g/2oz margarine
25g/1oz sugar
5g/1 tsp baking powder
125ml/4½oz milk

Filling
75g/3oz raspberry jam
350g/12oz raspberries, fresh, frozen or canned, drained
150ml/5 fl oz whipping cream, whipped
Icing sugar and mint sprigs for decorating

STEP 8

STEP 10

1. Preheat the oven to 220°C/425°F/Gas Mark 7.

2. Grease and line bases of two 18cm (7-inch) sandwich tins.

3. Sieve together the flour and baking powder and stir in the sugar. Cut the margarine into pieces and rub into the flour mixture until it resembles fine breadcrumbs.

4. Add the milk and mix together with a round bladed knife to form a soft dough.

5. Turn out onto a lightly floured surface and knead lightly, smoothing away cracks. Divide the scone dough in half and roll each into a circle about 18cm (7-inch) in diameter.

6. Place into prepared tins, press out to fit tins and brush with milk. Bake in pre-heated oven for 10 to 15 minutes until light golden brown in colour.

7. Carefully turn the scone rounds out onto a wire tray to cool and remove paper.

8. To complete the scone dessert, use a 12.5cm (5-inch) cutter or saucer, as a guide to cut the centre from one of the rounds with the baked side uppermost.

9. Turn the resulting ring over and spread with the jam. Place the second scone round onto a serving plate, and place the jam ring carefully on top.

10. Fill the centre of the scone round with the raspberries, reserving a few for decoration. Spoon, or pipe the whipped cream over the fruit.

11. Produce 8 equal triangles from the cut out disc and place them evenly on top of the cream, pointing towards the centre and at a slight angle.

12. Lightly dredge the scone dessert with icing sugar and refrigerate until served.

Cook's Notes

TIME: Preparation takes 30 minutes, baking takes 10-15 minutes.

SERVING IDEA: Decorate with the reserved raspberries just before serving to avoid discolouring the cream with their juice.

RICH FRUIT CAKE

A valuable standby for those unexpected guests who drop in for tea.

225g/8oz Homepride Self-Raising Flour
5g/1 tsp mixed spice
175g/6oz margarine
175g/6oz brown muscavado sugar
3 eggs, size 3
200g/7oz sultanas
100g/3½oz raisins
200g/7oz currants
100g/3½oz glace cherries, roughly chopped
50g/2oz mixed cut peel
Grated rind of 1 lemon

1. Preheat oven to 160°C/325°F/Gas Mark 3.

2. Grease and line a deep 18cm (7-inch) cake tin.

3. Sieve together the flour and mixed spice.

4. Cream the margarine and sugar together in a large mixing bowl until light and fluffy.

5. Beat in the eggs, one at a time, adding a little of the sieved flour with each egg.

STEP 5

6. Fold in the remaining flour and mixed spice followed by the prepared mixed fruit and lemon rind, mixing gently and thoroughly, until well incorporated.

STEP 6

7. Turn into the prepared tin and smooth the top.

STEP 7

8. Bake in the preheated oven for 1¾-2 hours, until a skewer, when inserted, comes out clean.

9. Leave in cake tin for 10 minutes. Turn out, remove paper and cool on a wire rack.

10. When cold, wrap in a double layer of greaseproof paper and store in a tin.

Cook's Notes

⏱ TIME: Preparation takes 25 minutes, baking takes 1 hour 45 minutes-2 hours.

👨‍🍳 COOK'S TIP: On removal from oven, brush surface with whole milk to give an attractive sheen.

◯ SERVING IDEAS: Store in an airtight container for at least 24 hours to mature before serving.

CHRISTMAS STOLLEN

This traditional German Christmas bread is a delightful addition to festive teas.

Starter
150g/5oz Harvest Gold Strong White Flour
12g/2 sachets Homepride Easy Blend Dried Yeast
100ml/3½oz fresh milk, well warmed

Dough
200g/7oz Harvest Gold Strong White Flour
40g/1½oz sugar
1 egg, size 3, separated
5g/1 tsp mixed spice
125g/4oz butter
50g/2oz marzipan, chopped finely

Fruit Mix
240g/8½oz sultanas
50g/2oz chopped almonds
75g/3oz mixed cut peel
15ml/1 tbsp water
25ml/1 fl oz rum

Glaze
15g/1 tbsp egg white
25ml/1oz fresh milk

1. Preheat oven to 190°C/375°F/Gas Mark 5.

2. Grease and line a 1kg (2lb) loaf tin with greaseproof paper.

3. To make the starter dough, sieve the flour into a large mixing bowl and stir in the yeast. Add the warm milk and work to a dough with a round bladed knife. Knead together for 3 minutes, cover and stand for 30 minutes in a warm place until double in size.

4. Meanwhile, prepare the dough by sieving together the remaining flour, mixed spice and sugar.

5. Rub in the butter and the marzipan until the mix resembles fine breadcrumbs. The resulting mix will be quite soft.

6. Knead the dough into the risen starter dough with the egg yolk for about 3 minutes until well mixed together.

7. Mix together the fruit ingredients and gradually knead this into the dough until well incorporated.

8. Allow to rest for about 10 minutes covered with lightly oiled cling film before rolling out on a floured surface to a rectangle 22 × 18cm (9 × 7 inches) with half being twice as thick as the other down the longer side.

9. Fold the thickest side of the dough over to just past the centre and roll the dough over. Carefully place the stollen into the prepared loaf tin.

10. Mix together the milk with the remaining egg white and glaze the stollen before baking in the preheated oven for 55 to 60 minutes until well risen and golden.

11. Cool on a wire rack and decorate with icing sugar when quite cold.

STEP 9

Cook's Notes

⏱ TIME: Preparation takes 60 minutes, baking takes 55-60 minutes.

👨‍🍳 COOK'S TIP: Glace cherries will colour the bread with a pink tinge.

◎ SERVING IDEAS: Can be served warm or leave in airtight tin for at least 24 hours to mature and serve in buttered slices.

PIZZA

Home-made pizza is always superior to its shop-bought counterparts.

Base
225g/8oz Harvest Gold Strong White Flour
2g/½ tsp salt
35g/1¼oz white shortening
6g/1 sachet Homepride Easy Blend Yeast
Pinch of white pepper
150ml/5 fl oz water (100ml cold, 50ml near
    boiling)

Topping
2 medium onions, peeled and sliced
1 garlic clove, peeled and crushed
227g/8oz canned, chopped tomatoes
10g/1 dessertspoon tomato purée
5g/1 tsp basil
5g/1 tsp oregano
Salt and black pepper to taste
225g/8oz cooked ham or chicken
1 red pepper, deseeded and sliced
125g/4oz grated Cheddar or Mozzarella cheese
6 stuffed olives, sliced

1. Preheat the oven to 180°C/350°F/Gas Mark 4.

2. Lightly grease a 30cm (12-inch) baking tray.

3. Sieve together 150g (5oz) of the flour with the salt and pepper and rub in the fat.

4. Mix in the yeast and blend in the warm water, beating well for about 3 minutes. Cover the bowl with cling film and stand in a warm place for 20 minutes until double in size.

5. Add the remaining 75g (3oz) flour to the proved dough and mix until it is well incorporated.

6. Turn the dough out onto a lightly floured surface and knead well for about 3 minutes. Allow to rest for 5 minutes covered with lightly oiled cling film.

7. Roll the dough out to a round about 30cm (12 inches) in diameter and place on the prepared baking tray.

8. In a saucepan, prepare the topping by heating together the onions, garlic, tomatoes, tomato purée, herbs and seasonings. Simmer uncovered for 5-10 minutes until slightly reduced and thickened.

9. Spread the tomato mixture on top of the prepared base to within 1 cm (½-inch) of the edge.

10. Chop half of the ham or chicken and place on top of the tomato mix with the sliced red pepper. Sprinkle over the grated cheese and bake in the preheated oven for about 25 to 30 minutes.

11. Meanwhile slice the remaining ham or chicken into strips, and immediately after removing the pizza from the oven, arrange the sliced meat in a lattice pattern on top of the cheese. Decorate with sliced olives and serve hot or cold.

STEP 11

Cook's Notes

⏱ TIME: Preparation takes about 1 hour. Baking takes about 15 minutes.

○ SERVING IDEA: Serve with a dressed green salad.

🍞 COOK'S TIP: Why not make two 6-inch pizzas out of the dough and freeze one, wrapped lightly in cling film or foil, for another day.

BUTTER SHORTCAKE BISCUITS

Makes approximately 20 biscuits

You'll have trouble resisting a biscuit tin full of these tasty treats.

200g/7oz Homepride Self-Raising Flour
125g/4oz butter, softened
75g/3oz caster sugar
2.5ml/½ tsp vanilla essence
25g/1oz cornflour

1. Preheat oven to 180°C/350°F/Gas Mark 4.

2. Grease a large baking tray.

3. Cream the butter and sugar together until light and fluffy. Add the vanilla essence.

4. Sieve together the self-raising flour and cornflour and fold into the creamed mixture. Mix to form a soft dough.

STEP 5

6. Place the biscuits on a baking tray about 2.5cm (1-inch) apart and prick each several times with a fork.

STEP 4

5. Roll the dough out on a floured surface to 0.5cm (¼-inch) thick and stamp out rounds using a 6cm (2½-inch) plain or fluted cutter.

STEP 6

7. Bake in preheated oven for about 15 minutes until light golden in colour.

8. Allow to cool slightly on the baking tray before placing the biscuits on a wire rack to cool completely. Store in an airtight container.

Cook's Notes

🕐 TIME: Preparation takes 15 minutes, cooking time takes 15 minutes.

👨‍🍳 COOK'S TIP: To stop cutter sticking to biscuit dough, dip into a little flour before stamping out each round.

⊙ SERVING IDEAS: Dust with a little icing sugar. Alternatively dip half of each biscuit into melted chocolate or pour chocolate over in a scattered line pattern.

YEASTED FRYING BATTER

This adaptable batter enhances sweet and savoury foods.

200g/7oz Homepride Plain White Flour
2.5g/½ tsp salt
25g/1oz margarine
6g/1 sachet Homepride Easy Blend Dried Yeast
75ml/3 fl oz milk
123ml/4 fl oz water
1 egg white

1. Sieve together the flour and salt and rub in the margarine.

2. Stir in the dried yeast.

3. Mix together the milk with the water and warm moderately. Add to the flour mixture and blend well together.

4. Cover and allow to stand in a warm place for about 30 minutes until the batter is frothy and well aerated.

5. Lightly whisk the egg white and fold into the batter.

STEP 5

6. Use to coat fish, vegetables, fruit etc. and then deep fry.

STEP 3

STEP 6

Cook's Notes

TIME: Preparation takes 15 minutes. Cooking time varies according to item being fried.

COOK'S TIP: If battering moist items, coat first in lightly seasoned Homepride plain flour before dipping in batter.

SERVING IDEAS: For fish, sprinkle with a little freshly squeezed lemon juice. For sweet fritters, sprinkle with a little caster sugar.

MILK BREAD PLAIT

An attractive bread, perfect for guests or special lunches.

Dough
450g/1lb Harvest Gold Strong White Flour
5g/1 tsp salt
15g/½oz butter
5g/1 tsp caster sugar
12g/2 sachets Homepride Easy Blend Yeast
290ml/10½ fl oz lukewarm milk

Glaze
1 egg, size 3, lightly beaten
50ml/2 fl oz milk
2.5g/½ tsp salt

1. Preheat oven to 190°C/375°F/Gas Mark 5.

2. Grease a baking tray.

3. Sieve together the flour and salt, and rub in the butter. Add yeast.

4. Dissolve sugar in the warm milk and mix in to form a soft dough.

5. Turn out onto a lightly floured surface and knead for about 5 minutes to give a smooth dough. Divide into three equal pieces and shape into rounds. Cover with lightly oiled cling film and rest for 5 minutes.

6. Roll each piece into a sausage shape. Pinch all three together at one end. Plait fairly tightly and pinch together at other end to seal. Place on the greased baking tray.

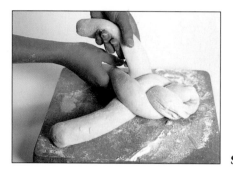

STEP 6

7. Beat together the egg with the milk and salt. Glaze the plait then cover with lightly oiled cling film, and allow to prove in a warm place for about 30 minutes until double in size.

8. Remove cling film, re-glaze and bake for 20 to 30 minutes until golden brown and well risen.

STEP 8

9. Place on a wire rack and re-glaze immediately for a shiny appearance. Cool completely before slicing.

Cook's Notes

⏱ TIME: Preparation takes 25 minutes, cooking takes 20-30 minutes.

👨‍🍳 COOK'S TIP: As a variation, when glazing before baking, sprinkle on some poppy seeds or sesame seeds.

⭕ SERVING IDEA: May be lightly toasted in slices as a type of milk rusk.

WHITE BLOOMER LOAF

Makes 2 small or 1 large loaf

This traditional loaf is perfect for all the family's needs.

Sponge
250g/9oz Harvest Gold Strong White Flour
5g/1 tsp caster sugar
6g/1 sachet Homepride Easy Blend Yeast
350ml/12 fl oz water (150ml almost boiling, 200ml cold)

Dough
250g/9oz Harvest Gold Strong White Flour
10g/2 tsps salt

Glaze
1 egg, size 3, lightly beaten
50ml/2 fl oz milk
2.5g/½ tsp salt

1. Preheat oven to 230°C/450°F/Gas Mark 8.

2. Lightly grease two baking trays.

3. Sieve together the first flour and sugar, and mix in the yeast. Add the water and mix to form a smooth batter. Cover and leave to prove in a warm place for about 30 minutes or until double in size.

4. Sieve together the second flour with the salt and add to the proved sponge. Mix to form a soft dough. Turn out onto a lightly floured surface and knead well for about 5 minutes until smooth.

5. Divide the dough in two and mould each half into bloomer shapes. Place each on baking trays with joins downwards.

STEP 4

6. Beat together the egg with the milk and salt and glaze the shaped dough. Cover with lightly oiled cling film and prove in a warm place until double in size.

7. Remove cling film, reglaze and score the top of each loaf with 5 evenly spaced diagonal cuts. Bake for 20 to 25 minutes until golden brown in colour and well risen.

STEP 7

8. Transfer to a wire rack and re-glaze immediately for a shiny appearance. Cool before slicing.

Cook's Notes

⏱ TIME: Preparation takes 25 minutes, baking takes 20-25 minutes.

🍴 COOK'S TIP: Scoring of the dough is best done with a very sharp, thin bladed knife.

⭕ SERVING IDEAS: Slice the loaf, spread generously with garlic butter and lightly grill.

WHITE BREAD

Makes one small 450g (1lb) loaf and five rolls or 1 large loaf

It's up to you whether you make rolls or loaves from this tasty dough.

500g/1lb 2oz Harvest Gold Strong White Flour
5g/1 tsp baking powder
5g/1 tsp salt
15g/½oz white vegetable fat
12g/2 sachets Homepride Easy Blend Dried Yeast
300ml/11 fl oz lukewarm water

Glaze
1 egg, size 3, lightly beaten
50ml/2 fl oz milk
2.5g/½ teaspoon salt

1. Preheat oven to 220°C/475°F/Gas Mark 8.

2. Grease a small loaf tin and a baking tray or a 1kg (2lb) loaf tin.

3. Sieve together the flour, baking powder and salt in a large bowl, and rub in the fat.

4. Mix in the yeast then blend in the water and mix to form a soft dough.

STEP 4

5. Turn out onto a lightly floured surface and knead for about 5 minutes to give a smooth dough.

STEP 5

6. Shape or mould as required, placing moulding joins downwards, ready for baking.

STEP 6

7. Beat together the egg with the milk and add the salt. Glaze the shaped dough with the egg wash and cover with lightly oiled cling film. Prove in a warm place until double in size.

8. Carefully remove the cling film, reglaze, and bake the rolls for about 10 minutes, the small loaf for 15 to 20 minutes and the large loaf for about 30 minutes, until well risen and golden brown.

9. Turn out onto a wire rack. Reglaze immediately with the egg and milk mixture for shiny appearance if desired.

10. Allow to cool before slicing.

Cook's Notes

TIME: Preparation takes 25 minutes, cooking takes up to 30 minutes.

COOK'S TIP: Always try to make bread in the warmest part of the kitchen and at the warmest time of day.

BROWN BREAD

Makes one small 450g (1lb) loaf and five rolls, or one large loaf

This bread is so good it only needs a touch of butter to be enjoyed at its best.

500g/1lb 2oz Harvest Gold Strong Brown Flour
5g/1 tsp salt
25g/1oz Trex (vegetable shortening)
5g/1 tsp baking powder
12g/2 sachets Homepride Easy Blend Yeast
5g/1 tsp caster sugar
300ml/11 fl oz water (150ml near boiling, 150ml cold)
Glaze
1 egg, size 3, lightly beaten
2.5g/½ tsp salt
50ml/2 fl oz milk

1. Preheat oven to 220°C/425°F/Gas Mark 7.

2. Grease a small loaf tin and baking tray or, for a large loaf, a 1kg (2lb) loaf tin.

3. Mix together the flour, baking powder and salt and rub in the fat. Add yeast.

STEP 4

4. Blend in the water and mix to form a soft dough.

5. Turn out onto a lightly floured surface and knead for about 5 minutes to give a smooth dough.

6. Shape or mould as required, placing mould joins downwards ready for baking.

STEP 6

7. Beat together the egg with the milk and salt. Brush the shaped dough with the egg glaze and cover with lightly oiled cling film. Prove in a warm place until double in size.

8. Remove the cling film, re-glaze, and bake the rolls for about 10 minutes, the small loaf for 15 to 20 minutes and the large loaf for about 20 to 30 minutes, until well risen and golden brown.

9. Turn out onto a wire rack and re-glaze immediately with egg mixture to give a shiny appearance.

10. Allow to cool before slicing.

Cook's Notes

TIME: Preparation takes 25 minutes, cooking takes up to 30 minutes.

SERVING IDEAS: Goes particularly well with starter dishes e.g. pâtés, fish and salads. Even better if still warm.

WHOLEMEAL DROP SCONES

Makes approximately 25

A delicious alternative to plain scones.

200g/7oz Harvest Gold Wholemeal Flour
15g/½oz baking powder
50g/2oz sugar
25g/1oz margarine
2 eggs, size 3
275ml/½ pint fresh milk
50g/2oz sultanas

1. Sieve the dry ingredients together in a large mixing bowl.

2. Rub the margarine into the flour mixture until it resembles fine breadcrumbs.

3. Whisk the eggs with the milk and add to the rubbed in mixture. Beat with a wire whisk or a spoon to a smooth, fairly thick batter consistency.

STEP 3

4. Lightly oil a large frying pan or griddle, place over a medium heat and allow to become moderately hot.

5. Drop 15ml (1 tbsp) of the batter onto the hot pan or griddle, about 5cm (2-inches) apart, and immediately sprinkle each with a few sultanas.

STEP 5

6. Cook the scones until bubbles appear on the top surface. Turn over and cook on the other side.

STEP 6

7. Continue with the remaining batter, wrapping the cooked scones in a clean tea towel to keep them warm and moist.

8. Serve hot or cold with butter.

Cook's Notes

TIME: Preparation takes 15 minutes, cooking takes 5 minutes.

COOK'S TIP: Stir a little cinnamon into the mixture or grate in some lemon or orange rind.

SERVING IDEAS: Before serving, scones may be cut with a fluted cutter and served with jam and cream or a sprinkling of sugar and cinnamon.

MINCEMEAT TARTS
WITH BUTTER PASTRY

Makes approximately 20

These delicious tarts shouldn't be reserved just for Christmas.

Pastry
225g/8oz Homepride Plain Flour
175g/6oz butter, cut into small pieces
15ml/1 tbsp caster sugar
1 egg, size 3, separated
½ orange, grated rind and juice
350g-450g/12oz-1lb mincemeat
30ml/2 tbsps brandy (optional)
Caster sugar to dust
Orange zest strips for decoration

1. Preheat oven to 200°C/400°F/Gas Mark 6.

2. To prepare the pastry, sieve the flour into a medium bowl and rub in the butter until the mixture resembles fine breadcrumbs.

3. Dissolve the caster sugar in the egg yolk with 10ml (2 tsps) orange juice. Add to the flour mixture with the grated rind of ½ an orange. Mix together with a round bladed knife to form a firm dough.

STEP 4

4. Turn out onto a lightly floured surface and knead lightly until smooth. Roll out the pastry to about 0.5cm (¼-inch) thick. Cut out about twenty rounds using a 7.5cm (3-inch) fluted cutter and twenty smaller rounds with a 5.5cm (2¼-inch) fluted cutter.

5. Line deep patty tins with the pastry, and place a heaped 5ml teaspoon of mincemeat, mixed with brandy if liked, into each base.

6. Dampen the edges of each tart and place the smaller rounds firmly in position on top of the pies. Seal well.

7. Lightly beat the remaining egg white and glaze each mincemeat tart, before making a small hole in the top of each using a skewer.

STEP 7

8. Bake in the preheated oven for about 15 minutes until light golden brown. Immediately sprinkle with caster sugar and orange zest strips, and leave to cool on a wire rack.

Cook's Notes

⏱ TIME: Preparation takes 25 minutes, baking takes 15 minutes.

◎ SERVING IDEAS: Carefully remove the lids and serve warm with brandy butter piped in the centre, then replace the lids.

🍴 COOK'S TIP: Use pastry trimmings to make holly and berry decorations. Cut out star shapes for the tops of pies for a more unusual appearance. Particularly suitable for freezing and reheating.

CHRISTMAS PUDDING

Christmas wouldn't be the same without a traditional home-made pudding.

65g/2½oz Homepride Plain Flour
10g/2 tsps mixed spice
65g/2½oz freshly made breadcrumbs
75g/3oz muscavado sugar
75g/3oz butter or margarine, melted
15g/1 level tbsp black treacle
2 eggs, size 3
60ml/4 tbsps old ale, stout or milk
Grated rind of ½ lemon
45g/1½oz flaked almonds
125g/4oz eating apples, peeled, cored and grated
50g/2oz mixed peel, chopped
50g/2oz raisins, seedless
150g/5oz currants
125g/4oz sultanas

1. Have ready a steamer two-thirds full of fast boiling water or a large saucepan with a tight-fitting lid, one-third full.

2. Grease and base line a 1.1 ltr (2-pint) pudding basin and a sheet of foil or greaseproof paper for the top.

3. Sieve together the flour and mixed spice in a large bowl and add the breadcrumbs and sugar.

4. Stir in the remaining ingredients and beat together well for about 3 minutes.

STEP 4

5. Turn mixture into prepared pudding basin and cover with the greased foil or greaseproof paper. Tuck in securely round the rim, or tie with string.

STEP 5

6. Steam for 6 hours, taking care to add more boiling water to the steamer as necessary.

7. Cool, re-cover with clean greaseproof paper and store in a cool, dry place.

8. To serve, steam for a further 2 to 3 hours. Remove from basin and flambé with brandy if desired.

Cook's Notes

TIME: Preparation takes 30 minutes, cooking takes 6 hours.

COOK'S TIP: Mix may be prepared one day, refrigerated, then steamed the following day. The mixture may be steamed in two 850ml (1½ pint) pudding basins, each taking 4 hours to steam.

SERVING IDEAS: Serve with tangerine and Cointreau butter as an alternative to brandy butter. Cream together 75g (3oz) unsalted butter and 75g (3oz) soft brown sugar. Beat in the grated rind of a small tangerine together with 15ml (1 tbsp) tangerine juice and a dash of Cointreau to taste.

STEAMED SYRUP SPONGE PUDDING

A heartening pudding which is perfect for cold winter days.

30ml/2 tbsps golden syrup
125g/4oz butter or margarine
125g/4oz caster sugar
2 eggs, size 3
175g/6oz Homepride Self-Raising Flour
Grated rind from ½ lemon
30ml/2 tbsps milk
Lemon slices and zest to garnish

1. Grease a 850ml (1½ pint) pudding basin and a double thickness of foil or greaseproof paper to cover the pudding.

2. Spoon the syrup into the bottom of the basin.

STEP 4

5. Carefully fold in the remaining flour and the milk using a metal spoon.

6. Place mixture into the pudding basin and smooth the top. Cover with the greased foil or greaseproof paper.

STEP 2

3. Cream together the butter or margarine and sugar until light and fluffy.

4. Beat in the eggs, one at a time adding a little of the flour with the second. Add the lemon rind.

STEP 6

7. Steam for 1½-2 hours, until the sponge has risen and springs back when lightly pressed. Turn out and serve hot, garnished with lemon slices and zest.

Cook's Notes

 TIME: Preparation takes 10 minutes, cooking takes 1½-2 hours.

COOK'S TIP: To prevent the golden syrup from sticking to the spoon, heat it in very hot water before spooning out syrup.

SERVING IDEAS: Squeeze fresh lemon juice over the pudding after turning out and portioning. Serve hot with fresh cream or custard.

SPOTTED DICK

A traditional dish which is just as popular today.

50g/2oz sultanas
50g/2oz currants
225g/8oz Homepride Self-Raising Flour
75g/3oz caster sugar
125g/4oz shredded suet
125ml/5 fl oz water

1. Wash dried fruits and dry on a clean tea towel.

2. Lightly grease a large sheet of foil or a double thickness of greaseproof paper.

3. In a large mixing bowl, stir together the dry ingredients and then add fruit.

4. Add the water and mix together to form a soft dough.

STEP 5

6. Wrap the dough loosely in the greased foil or greaseproof paper, securing the ends tightly.

STEP 4

5. Turn out onto a lightly floured board and form into a roll about 20cm (8-inches) long.

STEP 6

7. Steam for 1½-2 hours until the sponge has risen. Serve hot.

Cook's Notes

⏱ TIME: Preparation takes 20 minutes, cooking takes 1½-2 hours.

◻ SERVING IDEAS: Sprinkle with caster or granulated sugar and serve with custard.

👨‍🍳 COOK'S TIPS: For a vegetarian pudding use vegetable suet, available in most good supermarkets.

JAM SWISS ROLL

Excellent served with afternoon tea or as a dessert with cream.

65g/2½oz Homepride Self-Raising Flour
3 eggs, size 3
65g/2½oz caster sugar
Extra caster sugar for dredging (sieved)
45ml/3 tbsps jam, warmed
Strawberries to decorate

1. Preheat oven to 200°C/400°F/Gas Mark 6.

2. Grease and line a 28cm × 18cm (11-inch × 7-inch) Swiss roll tin with greaseproof paper.

3. Whisk together the eggs and sugar until they are light and creamy, and the whisk leaves a line when it is lifted out.

STEP 3

4. Carefully fold in the flour with a metal spoon.

5. Turn the mixture into the prepared tin and bake immediately for about 10 minutes until the cake springs back when lightly pressed.

STEP 5

6. Turn out onto a piece of greaseproof paper which has been dredged with caster sugar.

7. Cut a 0.5cm (¼-inch) strip from each of the long lengths of the Swiss roll. Spread with the warmed jam to within 0.5cm (¼-inch) of the edge and roll up quickly, keeping it wrapped in greaseproof paper. Allow to cool.

STEP 7

8. When cool, dredge with a little more caster sugar and decorate with fresh strawberries before serving.

Cook's Notes

⏱ TIME: Preparation takes 25 minutes, cooking takes 10 minutes.

🍴 COOK'S TIPS: Wet the blade of a palette knife in order to spread the mixture more easily and evenly in the baking tray prior to baking.

◯ SERVING IDEAS: Having trimmed the long edges of the Swiss roll, sprinkle sponge with a little lemon juice, roll up and allow to cool. When cold carefully unroll and fill with lemon curd and whipped cream, then re-roll.

RICH CHOCOLATE LAYER GATEAU

An extravagant treat which will delight your guests.

100g/3½oz Homepride Plain Flour
50g/2oz cocoa powder
50g/2oz butter
4 eggs, size 3
175g/6oz caster sugar

Syrup
175g/6oz sugar
150ml/¼ pint water
Tia Maria or coffee flavoured liqueur to taste

Filling and topping
365g/12½oz plain chocolate, chopped or grated
150ml/5 fl oz fresh whipping cream
30ml/2 tbsps brandy (optional)
Grated chocolate and chocolate shapes for
    decorating

1. Preheat oven to 180°C/350°F/Gas Mark 4.

2. Grease and base line a 20cm (8-inch) cake tin.

3. Sieve together the flour and cocoa powder. Melt the butter and allow to cool slightly.

4. Whisk together the eggs with the sugar until pale in colour and the whisk leaves a thick line when lifted out.

5. Using a metal spoon carefully fold in half of the sieved flour and cocoa, then pour in a thin stream of melted butter at the side of the bowl. Fold in remaining flour.

6. Pour the cake mixture into the prepared tin and bake in the preheated oven for 30-40 minutes, until well risen and spongy to the touch.

7. Allow to cool slightly before turning out onto a wire rack and removing the lining paper. When quite cold slice the cake horizontally into 3 layers.

8. To make the moistening syrup, gently boil together the sugar and water for about 3 minutes, until the sugar is dissolved. Cool and add the Tia Maria. Pour the prepared syrup liberally over the top surface of each slice of cake.

9. To prepare the chocolate filling, melt the chocolate in a bowl over a pan of simmering water, and gradually add the fresh cream whilst whisking continuously. Allow to cool then whisk well until smooth.

STEP 9

10. Sandwich the three moistened layers of the gateau together with the chcolate filling, allowing about 45ml (3 tbsps) for each layer. Using a palette knife, carefully cover the sides and top of the cake with the remaining chocolate mixture.

11. Decorate the gateau with grated chocolate and shapes before serving.

Cook's Notes

TIME: Preparation takes 45 minutes, cooking takes 30 to 40 minutes.

COOK'S TIP: Chill the chocolate base before slicing horizontally into three with a bread knife.

SERVING IDEAS: For an extra special treat serve with whipped cream or ice cream. Delicious served slightly warmed – heat individual servings for a few seconds in the microwave.

FRESH CREAM CHOCOLATE ROULADE

This dessert is simple to prepare yet impressive enough for dinner parties.

3 eggs, size 3
65g/2½oz caster sugar
50g/2oz Homepride Self-Raising Flour
15g/½oz cocoa powder

Filling
50g/2oz caster sugar
50ml/2 fl oz water
50g/2oz plain chocolate, grated
150ml/5 fl oz whipping cream, whipped
Icing sugar for dusting
Whipped double cream and chocolate shapes to
    decorate

1. Preheat oven to 200°C/400°F/Gas Mark 6.

2. Grease and line a 28cm × 18cm (11-inch × 7-inch) Swiss roll tin with greaseproof paper.

3. Whisk together the eggs and sugar until they are light and creamy, and the whisk leaves a line when lifted out.

4. Sieve in the flour and cocoa and carefully fold in with a metal spoon.

5. Spread the mixture into the prepared tin and bake immediately for about 10 minutes until the sponge springs back when lightly pressed.

6. Cover with a sheet of greaseproof paper and a damp tea towel and leave until completely cold.

7. Meanwhile prepare the filling by gently heating together the sugar and water until the sugar has dissolved. Bring to the boil, remove from the heat and stir in the grated chocolate until melted.

8. Turn the cooled roulade out onto a piece of greaseproof paper which has been dusted with icing sugar.

9. Remove the lining and cut a 0.5cm (¼-inch) strip from each end of the long lengths of the sponge.

10. Spread with the hot chocolate sauce to within 0.5cm (¼-inch) of the edge and allow the sauce to soak in slightly. Cover with a rectangle of greaseproof paper and carefully roll up the roulade. Allow the chocolate sauce to cool completely.

11. When the chocolate filling is quite cold, gently unroll the sponge and remove the greaseproof paper. Spread the whipped cream on top of the chocolate to within 0.5cm (¼-inch) of the edge, and re-roll the roulade.

STEP 11

12. Dust with more icing sugar if required. Pipe cream around edges and place chocolate shapes between rosettes.

Cook's Notes

⌛ TIME: Preparation takes 35 minutes, baking takes 10 minutes.

◻ SERVING IDEAS: Fold chopped pears which have been soaked in Kirsch, into the whipped cream filling.

BUTTER MADEIRA CAKE

A year-round favourite, popular with all age groups.

175g/6oz butter
175g/6oz caster sugar
2 eggs, size 3
225g/8oz Homepride Self-Raising Flour
30ml/2 tbsps milk
5ml/1 tsp lemon juice

1. Preheat oven to 160°C/325°F/Gas Mark 3.

2. Grease and line a 18cm (7-inch) round cake tin.

3. Cream the butter and sugar together in a mixing bowl until light and fluffy.

STEP 3

4. Beat in the eggs, one at a time, adding a little of the sieved flour with each egg.

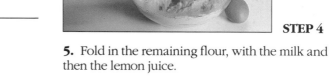

STEP 4

5. Fold in the remaining flour, with the milk and then the lemon juice.

6. Place mixture into the prepared tin and smooth the top.

7. Bake on the centre shelf of the pre-heated oven for about 1¼ hours until a skewer, when inserted, comes out clean.

STEP 6

8. Allow to stand in tin for 5 minutes before turning out. Remove paper and cool on a wire tray.

Cook's Notes

🕐 TIME: Preparation takes 20 minutes, cooking takes 1 hour 15 minutes.

🍞 COOK'S TIP: Place a piece of citron peel gently on top of the cake, halfway through cooking for extra lemon flavour.

◯ SERVING IDEAS: Use left over week old Madeira cake for trifles, spread with jam or marmalade and moisten with sherry or Madeira wine.

CHOCOLATE CHIP COOKIES

Makes approximately 20

Children love these satisfying biscuits.

150g/5oz butter, softened
125g/4oz caster sugar
1 egg, size 3, lightly beaten
Vanilla essence to taste
225g/8oz Homepride Self-Raising Flour
75g/3oz Homepride Plain Flour
100g/3½oz plain chocolate drops or finely
   chopped plain chocolate

1. Preheat oven to 220°C/425°F/Gas Mark 7.

2. Cream butter and sugar together until light and fluffy.

3. Beat in the egg gradually, together with the vanilla essence.

4. Sieve together the two flours and fold into the creamed mixture.

STEP 5

6. Turn out onto a lightly floured surface and roll the dough into a sausage shape about 2½cm (1-inch) thick, cut the roll of dough into slices 2cm (¾-inch) thick, place on a baking tray and flatten to about 5cm (2 inches) in diameter.

STEP 6

7. Bake in preheated oven for 10 minutes until light golden brown in colour.

8. Remove from baking tray with a palette knife and leave to cool on a wire rack.

STEP 4

5. Stir in the chocolate drops until well mixed through the dough.

Cook's Notes

⏲ TIME: Preparation takes 10 minutes, cooking takes 10 minutes.

◯ SERVING IDEAS: When just out of the oven, sprinkle with caster sugar for a crunchy topping.

🎩 COOK'S TIP: If using a bar of chocolate, leave to soften slightly in a warm place before chopping, then chill well until required.

FRUIT CRUMBLE

This adaptable dish is given extra taste by the addition of sultanas and nuts.

450g/1lb prepared fresh fruit, frozen or canned (drained)
275ml/½ pint juices from fruit and water
10g/1 dessertspoon cornflour
Sugar to taste

Topping
200g/7oz Homepride Plain Flour
100g/3⅓oz porridge oats
100g/5oz butter
100g/3½oz granulated sugar
25g/1oz sultanas
25g/1oz walnuts or hazelnuts, chopped
Fresh fruit and mint leaves to decorate

1. Preheat oven to 180°C/350°F/Gas Mark 4.

2. Lightly grease an 850ml (1½ pint) pie dish.

3. To prepare the fruit filling if using fresh fruit, lightly simmer in a little water until just tender. Drain, reserving the juice, and place in the pie dish.

4. Make the drained fruit juice up to 275ml (½ pint) with water and gradually add to the cornflour.

5. Pour into a saucepan and slowly bring to the boil stirring continuously. Add sugar to taste and stir until dissolved.

6. Carefully pour over the prepared fruit in the pie dish.

7. Prepare the crumble topping by mixing

STEP 7

together the flour and porridge oats. Rub in the butter.

8. Stir in the sugar, sultanas and nuts, and mix well.

9. Pile the crumble mixture over the fruit to completely cover.

STEP 9

10. Bake in preheated oven for 40 minutes until the crumble is golden brown and thoroughly heated. Decorate with fresh fruit and mint before serving.

Cook's Notes

⏱ TIME: Preparation takes about 25 minutes, cooking takes 40 minutes.

◎ SERVING IDEAS: Serve hot with dairy ice cream or whipped fresh cream if served cold.

👨‍🍳 COOK'S TIP: Save time by preparing fruit and topping separately beforehand, chill, put together and bake next day.

BAKED JAM ROLL

Use your favourite jam for this classic treat.

175g/6oz Homepride Self-Raising Flour
15g/1 tbsp caster sugar
Pinch of salt
75g/3oz butter or margarine
30ml/2 tbsps milk
125g/4oz jam

Glaze
Milk for brushing
Sugar for dredging
Fruit slices for decoration

1. Preheat oven to 200°C/400°F/Gas Mark 6.

2. Grease and line a 450g (1lb) loaf tin with greaseproof paper.

3. Sieve the flour with the caster sugar and salt, and rub in the butter or margarine until the mixture resembles fine breadcrumbs.

4. Add the milk and mix to a soft dough.

STEP 4

5. Turn out onto a lightly floured surface and knead lightly until smooth. Roll out to a rectangle

18cm (7-inches) and 22cm (9-inches) and spread with jam to within 2.5cm (1-inch) of the edge. Brush the edge with milk.

STEP 5

6. Roll the dough up so that the finished roll is 18cm (7-inches) long, seal the edges and place in the prepared tin.

STEP 6

7. Bake in the preheated oven for 40 minutes.

8. Brush with milk and sprinkle with sugar. Serve hot decorated with fruit slices.

Cook's Notes

TIME: Preparation takes 20 minutes, cooking takes 40 minutes.

COOK'S TIP: When rolling pastry out, keep baking tin nearby for use as a guide to the size required.

SERVING IDEAS: When baked, apply generous layer of icing sugar on crust and return to oven to give shiny finish. Serve hot with custard and cream.

WHOLEMEAL SAVOURY CURD CHEESE AND BROCCOLI QUICHE

This unusual quiche is perfect for summer picnics.

Pastry
200g/7oz Homepride Self-Raising Wholemeal
    Flour
2.5g/½ tsp salt
Pinch of black pepper
125g/4oz margarine
50g/2 fl oz water

Filling
200g/7oz blanched broccoli spears
225g/8oz curd cheese (low fat)
2 eggs, size 3
50ml/2 fl oz milk
2.5g/½ teaspoon salt
Pinch of black pepper
Parsley sprigs for garnish

1. Preheat oven to 200°C/400°F/Gas Mark 6.

2. Mix together the flour with the salt and pepper. Cut the margarine into small pieces and add to the flour. Rub in with fingertips until the mixture resembles fine breadcrumbs.

3. Add the water and mix together with a round bladed knife to form a soft dough. Turn out on a lightly floured surface and knead until smooth.

4. Roll out a round large enough to line a 20cm (8-inch) flan ring placed on a baking sheet. Lift the pastry carefully on the rolling pin and ease into the ring without breaking. Press smoothly round sides and bottom. Cut off surplus pastry with a sharp knife.

5. Line the inside of the pastry case with a round of greaseproof paper and arrange baking beans or

crusts of bread on top to prevent pastry rising. Bake for 15 minutes in the preheated oven.

STEP 4

STEP 5

6. Remove greaseproof paper and beans and reduce oven temperature to 190°C/375°F/Gas Mark 5.

7. To prepare the filling lay the broccoli evenly over the base of the pastry case. Lightly beat together the eggs with the milk, cheese and seasoning. Pour over the broccoli and bake for 15 to 20 minutes until the filling is set.

8. Serve hot or cold garnished with parsley.

Cook's Notes

TIME: Total preparation and cooking time is 1 hour 45 mins.

SERVING IDEAS: Serve with a mixed tossed salad and new potatoes.

COOK'S TIP: For that extra piquance, sprinkle the inside of the blind baked pastry shell with some Worcester sauce before adding the filling.

FRUIT BREAD AND BUN DOUGH

Makes one small 450g (1lb) loaf and 10 rolls, or one large loaf

This traditional recipe produces perfect results.

500g/1lb 2oz Harvest Gold Strong White Flour
10g/2 tsps baking powder
25g/1oz margarine
12g/2 sachets Homepride Easy Blend Yeast
40g/1½oz caster sugar
300ml/11 fl oz water (150ml near boiling,
   150ml cold)
250g/9oz currants and/or sultanas (optional)

Glaze
1 egg, size 3, lightly beaten
50ml/2 fl oz milk

1. Preheat the oven to 220°C/425°F/Gas Mark 7.

2. Grease a small loaf tin and a baking tray or a 1kg (2lb) loaf tin.

3. Sieve together the flour and baking powder in a large bowl and rub in the margarine. Add yeast.

4. Dissolve the caster sugar in the lukewarm water and add to form a soft dough. Turn out onto a lightly floured surface and knead for about 5 minutes to give a smooth, firm dough.

5. To incorporate the fruit, break the dough into small pieces and knead in the currants or sultanas, until evenly distributed throughout the dough.

6. Divide the dough in half and mould one half to fit the 450g (1lb) loaf tin. Form 10 small rounds with the remaining mix and place on the greased baking tray 1.5cm (½-inch) apart. Alternatively, mould all of the dough into a 1kg (2lb) loaf tin.

STEP 5

7. Beat together the egg with the milk and use to glaze the loaf and buns. Cover with lightly oiled cling film and prove until about double in size.

8. Carefully remove the cling film, re-glaze with egg and milk and bake the small loaf for 20 to 25 minutes, the buns for 8 to 10 minutes or the large loaf for 30 to 35 minutes, until well risen and golden brown. The loaf and buns should sound hollow when gently tapped on the base.

STEP 8

9. Turn out and cool on a wire rack.

Cook's Notes

⏱ TIME: Preparation takes about 45 minutes, baking takes up to 35 minutes.

🎩 COOK'S TIP: For a well risen but softer crust, place a large tin of hot water in the base of the oven before baking.

⭕ SERVING IDEAS: Glaze loaf and buns with a light syrup immediately after removing from the oven. Boil together 30ml/2 tbsps sugar with 45ml/3 tbsps water for 1-2 minutes without stirring. Alternatively coat with glacé icing when cold.

ICED BAKEWELL TART

An old recipe still much loved today.

Pastry
150g/5oz Homepride Plain Flour
60g/2½oz butter
1 yolk from size 3 egg
15g/1 tbsp caster sugar
15g/1 tbsp cold water

Filling
75g/3oz butter or margarine, softened
75g/3oz caster sugar
2 eggs, size 3
75g/3oz ground almonds
½ grated rind and juice of fresh lemon
1 egg white from pastry above
75g/3oz raspberry jam

Glace Icing
100g/4oz sieved icing sugar
20ml/4 tsps hot water
Freshly squeezed lemon juice to taste
Toasted, flaked almonds to decorate

1. Preheat the oven to 190°C/375°F/Gas Mark 5.

2. Sieve the flour into a medium bowl and rub in the butter until it resembles fine breadcrumbs.

3. Mix together the egg yolk with the caster sugar and add to the rubbed in mixture along with enough water to form a soft dough.

4. Turn out onto a lightly floured surface and knead gently until smooth and silky. Roll out the pastry to fit an 18cm (7-inch) flan ring placed on a baking tray.

5. Lift the pastry carefully on the rolling pin and ease into the ring without breaking. Press smoothly round sides and bottom. Cut off surplus pastry with

a sharp knife. Chill in the refrigerator whilst making the filling.

6. Cream together the butter or margarine and the sugar until light and fluffy. Add the eggs one at a time, followed by the egg white, beating well after each addition.

7. Fold in the ground almonds with the lemon rind (zest) and juice.

8. Spread the jam evenly over the base of the pastry case then spoon the bakewell filling mix on top. Smooth the surface.

STEP 8

9. Bake in the preheated oven for 35 to 40 minutes until golden brown and firm to the touch. Allow to cool before removing from the flan ring.

10. To prepare the iced topping, place the hot water into a small bowl. Slowly add the sieved icing sugar, stirring well to give a smooth icing. When all the sugar has been incorporated, beat well.

11. Add enough lemon juice to taste then spread the icing over the top surface of the baked tart, and allow to set before serving. Decorate with toasted almonds.

Cook's Notes

TIME: Preparation takes 35 minutes, cooking takes 35 to 40 minutes.

SERVING IDEAS: Serve warm with whipped cream or custard.

SAVOURY FILLED PANCAKES

This tasty mix of ingredients makes the perfect lunch or supper dish.

Pancake
125g/4oz Homepride Plain Flour
1 egg, size 3, lightly beaten
150ml/5 fl oz milk
150ml/5 fl oz water
25g/1oz butter, melted

Filling
125g/4oz smoked streaky bacon, chopped
50g/2oz onion, peeled and chopped
125g/4oz chicken livers, washed, dried and finely chopped
225g/8oz spinach, cooked and chopped
60g/2½oz Parmesan cheese, grated
1 egg, size 3, lightly beaten
Salt and freshly ground black pepper

Sauce
50g/2oz butter
50g/2oz Homepride Plain Flour
575ml/1 pint milk
50g/2oz Bel Paese cheese, grated
Salt and white pepper
French flat leaf parsley to garnish

1. To prepare the pancakes, sieve flour into a medium mixing bowl and beat in the egg and milk for 3 minutes until smooth and light.

2. Gradually whisk in the water, and pour in the melted butter in a thin stream. Beat lightly until well mixed.

3. Make pancakes in a medium-sized frying pan or omlette pan. Preheat the oven to 190°C/375°F/Gas Mark 5.

4. To make the filling, fry together the bacon and the onions until lightly browned. Stir in the chicken livers and cook, stirring, for a further 3 minutes.

5. Add the spinach and Parmesan cheese and heat through. Remove from the heat and beat in the egg. Add seasoning to taste.

6. Place a generous amount of mixture across the centre of each pancake and roll up. Place in the base of a large, lightly buttered ovenproof dish, then prepare the sauce.

7. Melt the butter over a moderate heat in a medium saucepan and stir in the flour. Cook, stirring continuously for 1 to 2 minutes.

8. Remove from the heat and gradually add the milk. Return to the heat and, stirring continuously, bring to the boil and simmer over a low heat for 2 to 3 minutes. Add the cheese and stir until melted.

9. Season to taste then pour over the prepared pancakes. Bake in the preheated oven for 25 minutes until thoroughly heated. Serve garnished with French parsley.

Cook's Notes

⏱ TIME: Preparation of the pancakes, filling and bechamel sauce takes around 90 minutes. Cooking finished dish takes 25 minutes.

👨‍🍳 COOK'S TIP: Pancakes may be made in advance and frozen, interleaved with greaseproof paper. Allow to thaw for 2 hours at room temperature.

◯ SERVING IDEAS: Sprinkle with grated cheese and breadcrumbs before baking for a crunchy topping.

INDEX

Photography by Peter Barry
Recipes Prepared and Styled by Helen Burdett
Designed by Judith Chant
Edited by Jillian Stewart